ART ACROSS THE WORLD

Marshall Cavendish Books, London W1

Marshall Cavendish Books Limited
58 Old Compton Street, London W1

First published 1969
© Marshall Cavendish Limited 1968
© Marshall Cavendish Books Limited 1969

This book may not be sold in the U.S.A. or Canada
Printed by Proost, Turnhout, Belgium
462 00250 0

Picture credits

(T = Top B = Bottom L = Left R = Right C = Centre)

Contents

Introduction
by Bernard L. Myers
Associate of the Royal College of Art

WESTERN MUSEUMS are not only full of great works of art but display in solemn and precious isolation many things that were once part of everyday life. Works of art in the West now have very little significance in the average person's life, whether secular or religious. Art is an extra, a kind of luxury associated with off-duty leisure; a means of escape from and a barrier against the boredom and plainness of the everyday world.

Both our museums and private collectors have been acquiring works of art from outside Western culture for some time past. We are learning to appreciate strange art forms much more than we used to, and films and television programmes have done much to arouse curiosity about people, places and ideas outside our own familiar world.

We still nevertheless tend to look at exotic art, both from far lands, as in the case of Africa and the Orient, or another time, as in the case of Pre-Columbian America, as we look at our own art. We try to find familiar recognisable forms, and look for the pleasures of line, or colour, or even strangeness, on the level of excitement of the senses, and perhaps as an alternative to our own art made over familiar by the various means of reproduction.

In most cases, however, these arts still form part of everyday life. They are pictures or objects for use, not simply decoration or a collector's pride or as relief from reality. They are signs and symbols which have as powerful social and religious meanings for their creators and their public as our traffic signs have for us. Without some explanation of meaning, of how and why these often complex and strange forms are or were made, we are only getting a fraction of possible enjoyment from them.

Since, for most of us, arts of other cultures still mean visits to museums, or travel films, or television programmes, a more systematic guide, well illustrated and to which we can refer at leisure both to discover and to recall, is essential. This book tells us about and shows us with many colour illustrations, these arts in their settings and with their peoples, from India, China and Japan, from the Islamic lands of the Middle East, the ritual and magic of Africa, and the Indian cultures of Central America.

Sensual and holy, the art of India

Temples hewn from rock, rhythmic and vital figure studies - the inventive and joyous art of India is a 4,000-year story in which human beauty and religious faith achieve a unique harmony.

DEEP SYMBOLIC MEANING permeates the whole of Indian art, fusing the twin themes of sex and religion in harmonious combination. India (including both present-day India and Pakistan) has been one of the most fertile sources of artistic inspiration for an unbroken period of more than 2,000 years, but its earliest art treasures are at least 4,000 years old. The subcontinent has produced an amazing variety of styles in painting, sculpture and architecture, reflecting the taste of immigrant settlers whose art has been blended into the mixed culture of the country.

Rhythm and vitality

Between about 2500 BC and 1500 BC, a pre-Aryan civilization flourished at Harrapa, Mohenjo-Daro, and other cities of the Indus valley. Seals, statues, jewellery and pottery excavated from the Indus cities resemble remains from Sumerian cities, suggesting that an interchange of artistic ideas existed in earliest-known times. The bronze figurine of an impish dancing girl has the rhythm and vitality which charac-terized the whole of Indian sculpture for the following 3,000 years.

Little is known about art, or indeed history, in India between the disappearance of the Indus civilization and the rise of Buddhism, which flourished during the reign of King Asoka (272–232 BC). The Buddhists built huge brick *stupas* (domed monuments capped by wooden or stone umbrellas) as shrines to contain sacred relics of the Buddha and Buddhist saints. The stupas were surrounded by railed passageways round which Buddhists ceremonially trudged in devotion to the Buddha. The first stupas were probably modelled on the pattern of earlier burial mounds erected over the remains of dead chiefs and kings. The balustrade posts of an early stupa (second century BC), at Bharhut (near Allahabad), are lavishly decorated with *Yakshas* and *Yakshis* (male and female imps) and with worshippers adoring symbols of the Buddha.

But perhaps the most interesting stupa is at Sanchi, near Bhopal. The Sanchi balustrade has four finely carved gateways which illustrate stories of the Buddha

architecture' by cutting caves into the rock face and sculpting them into monasteries complete with assembly chambers, cells and stupas. Karli and Ajanta, in Maharashtra state, are good examples of these cave-monasteries. Karli, which dates from the second century BC, is carved 124 feet into the rock. Its doorway is flanked by sensual pairs of lovers, representative of the whole of Indian temple sculpture. At Ajanta, Buddhist monks cut 28 cave-monasteries during the first seven centuries AD, and developed a flourishing school of Buddhist painting.

The slim waist, wide hips and full bust of a *Yakshini*, or tree-goddess, exemplify the ideal of female beauty held in the second century A. D.

The bronze dancing girl, *above,* was fashioned at Mohenjo-Daro nearly 4,500 years ago, but her character and vitality make her appeal timeless.

from the *Jataka Tales* (a collection of about 500 popular stories of the Buddha's lives on Earth). The Sanchi sculptors had a remarkable insight into plant and animal forms. Early Buddhist sculptors never showed the Buddha in human form. They represented him instead by symbols that included wheels, alms bowls, empty thrones, footprints and sandals. But in the ornate stupa at Amaravati (completed about AD 200) sculptors caught the intensity of religious passion in some of the first carvings of the Buddha in human form.

The Buddhists developed 'rock-cut

Simultaneously with the development of stupa architecture, new styles of sculpture emerged at Mathura and at Gandhara in northern India. It was at one or other of these centres that sculptors produced the first images of the Buddha in conventional postures, showing him protecting, meditating, praying, preaching, warning, blessing, and so on, according to the position of his right hand. The Mathura style, which began possibly as early as the end of the first century BC, was wholly Indian, and both Jainism and Buddhism influenced its development. The Mathura sculptors produced many plaques of medi-

Torso of a Bodhisattva, fifth century. Subtle modelling and perfect blending of stylistic figures shows the mastery of Gupta sculptors.

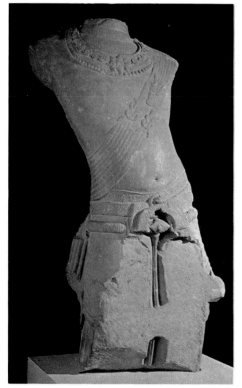

At Ellora, the great temple of Kailasanatha was hewn from vast masses of solid rock. It is a splendid example of 'rock-cut' architecture.

tating Jain saints, but their themes were sometimes less austere. They blended the pious harmoniously with the sensual. Their Yakshis have the same seductive appeal as the Mohenjo-Dara dancing girl created more than 2,000 years before. Gandhara art was Greco-Buddhist in style and began about the first century BC as a by-product of trading links between the Roman empire and northwestern India. The Gandhara craftsmen portrayed the Buddha, bodhisattvas and various Indian deities almost in the image of Greco-Roman deities.

The earliest existing Indian paintings

are at Ajanta, painted in the first seven centuries AD by Buddhist artists who worked on the interior walls of the cave-monasteries by sunlight reflected from metal mirrors. The painters took both sacred and secular subjects for their themes. Along with scenes from the Buddha's previous lives, they impartially depicted princes and beggars, coolies and peasants, ascetic saints and bejewelled courtesans.

Inspired by Buddhist artists and builders, Jains and Hindus, too, developed rock architecture. Buddhists, Jains and Hindus cut 34 adjacent cave temples into the rock at Ellora (near Ajanta) between the fifth and eighth centuries AD. But the most marvellous achievement of the rock-cutters at Ellora was the great Temple of Kailasanatha, built by the Hindus in the eighth century AD. The site of this vast temple is 164 feet long and 96 feet high. The whole structure – chambers, stairways, pillars, gateways and statues – was carved out from solid rock.

Exotic temple sculptures

The Hindus built a beautiful group of temples at Khajuraho (about 100 miles southeast of Jhansi), in the tenth and eleventh centuries. The convex temple towers taper upwards for the whole of their height (about 100 feet), so that the whole group looks like a range of miniature mountains. But the Khajuraho temples are admired not so much for their architecture as for their lavish, delectably carved erotic sculptures. Other beautiful temples, also elaborately sculptured, are the Lingaraja temple at Bhubanasar, dedicated to Siva, and the Sun Temple at Konarak, both in Orissa state.

Dravidian people of southern India built massive granite temples from the eleventh and twelfth centuries onwards. The focal points of each temple site are the intricately sculptured *gopurams* (tapered towers) that stand over the main gateways.

Each temple stood at the centre of a city, and the four main streets began at the main gateways of the temple. The great Madurai temple, built in the seventeenth century, is perhaps the most impressive of these structures. The gopuram over the south gate is covered for its entire height with sculptured figures in human form, arranged in tiers as though sitting in boxes at the theatre. The walled site of the largest Indian temple, at Srirangam is about half a mile square. Six inner walls, each topped by sculptured gopurams, enclose the inner shrine.

2,000 years of metalwork

The Tamils of southern India produced outstanding artistic metalwork in the

Indians clasp their hands behind their backs round the famous Iron Pillar at Delhi to obtain good luck. It was cast in AD 400, but not until the nineteenth century could Europeans attempt a similar feat.

tenth and eleventh centuries. Indian metalwork is in fact very old. The Iron Pillar, a memorial erected at Delhi about AD 400, stands more than 23 feet high. It has technological rather than artistic interest. But it provides evidence of the skill of ancient India's iron-founders and metallurgists, for no single piece of iron of such size could have been produced in Europe until the middle of the nineteenth century. Although completely exposed in a monsoon climate it remains rustless.

Small works of artistic metal-ware have been produced in India for about 2,000 years. The Tamils became specialists in producing graceful bronze figures of the four-armed Siva as Lord of the Dance, encircled in a ring of fire. In these conventional Siva bronzes, one foot mounts a crushed demon, the other swirls with body and arms in the frenzy of an ecstatic dance. Siva and other subjects of the bronzes were usually modelled in wax, which was then covered with clay. The wax was then melted off, to leave a mould into which molten metal was poured.

The Hindus cast or sculpted their gods and goddesses according to conventional basic forms. They were, however, allowed sufficient freedom to create a variety of detail within the basic conventions. The wealthy Jains added distinctive styles and techniques to India's sculpture-architecture. Their marble temples at Mount Abu, in Rajastan state, have a gayer appearance than the heavier Hindu structures. One of these, Vimala, dedicated to their first *tirthankara* (legendary teacher of a past era), is full of fascinating sculptures depicting Jain mythological scenes. Giant nude tirthankaras, carved from the rock face at Gwalior in the fifteenth century, stare impassively into the distance, remote from the affairs of this world.

In the early thirteenth century, Kutub-ud-din, a Moslem conqueror, from Afghanistan, became the first Sultan of Delhi. Surprisingly, the great Kutub Minar (238 feet), a fluted minaret of marble and sandstone completed in 1231–32, was named not after him but after a migrant from Baghdad. The early Moslems contributed practically nothing to painting and sculp-

The Kutub Minar, in memory of a thirteenth-century Moslem conqueror's victory is built of marble and sandstone and is 238 feet high.

9

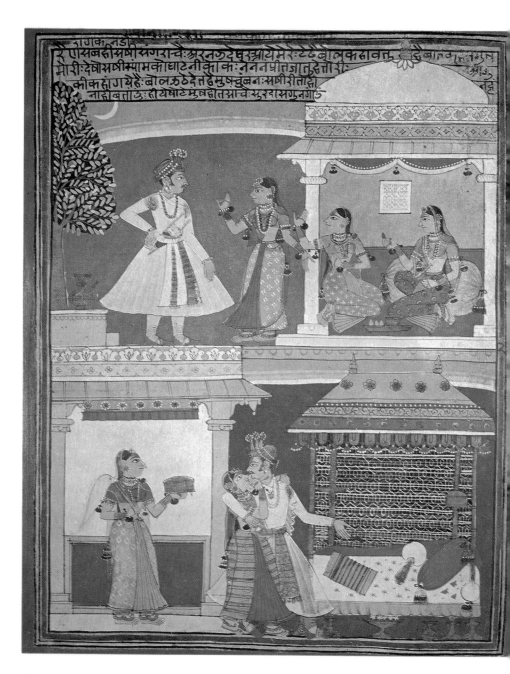

ture because their religion barred image-making. But they introduced mosque architecture, particularly the dome and minaret, into India. Their traditional architectural styles gradually became 'Indianized' because Hindu craftsmen constructed their buildings.

More waves of invaders passed over northern India, and in 1526, Baber, a dispossessed part-Mongol Chaghatai Turkish king, established himself as *Mughal*

Completed in 1654, the Taj Mahal, described as coming 'within more measurable distance of perfection than any other work of man'.

(Mongol Moslem) emperor of India. Whereas in pre-Moslem India the Hindus had employed their architectural talent on temples, the Mughals also built splendid palaces and private tombs. Shah Jahan (ruled 1628–58) built the white marble Taj Mahal at Agra as a magnificent tomb for his most favoured wife. About 20,000 craftsmen worked on it for more than 20 years. Mughal architecture in India is decorated with beautiful calligraphy, and floral designs adapted from Italian motifs. Carved screens of alabaster or marble are special features of Mughal buildings. The Sikhs, who emerged as a separate sect in the fifteenth century, combined Hindu and Moslem ideas in both their religion and their art. The outstanding example of their architecture is the Golden Temple set in a pool

Artists painted their miniatures to please the wealthy men who paid them, and took secular rather than religious themes for their subjects. They painted innumerable portraits, and illustrated books with animal and bird pictures. When the Mughal empire began to disintegrate in the early eighteenth century, Mughal art declined.

Themes from epic, myth and music

Meanwhile, Hindu art had gained a new lease of life. Under the patronage of the princes of Rajputana, *Rajput* painters evolved a new style of miniatures, taking religious stories, myths and epics as their themes. The Rajput painters applied Mughal techniques to Hindu themes. The flirtations of the flute-playing god Krishna (conventionally blue-skinned) with the *gopis* (milkmaids) provided a fairly typical subject. The Rajput artists also looked to music for themes, and painted *Raga-Ragini* pictures to represent musical modes. Women dominate all Rajput painting. The sophisticated sensuousness of women painted by the Buddhists more than a thousand years earlier, contrasts with the Rajputs' characterless, lotus-eyed heroines whose faces showed no emotion but whose passion was conveyed by gestures and symbols.

Several schools of painting which derived from Mughal-Rajput art flourished in the Punjab and the northwest of India. Collectively they are called the *Kangra valley* School. The Kangra valley artists painted princely scenes in wonderfully glowing colours. Their women are altogether more convincing, more sophisticated, than the women of the Rajasthan painters. Kangra valley painters again remind us that Indians are the experts in the art and science of love, which they see as being of two main kinds: love in separation, and love together. In Kangra valley 'love in separation' paintings, various birds and animals represent absent mates. Lightning and storm clouds symbolize

A Mughal miniature, *c.* 1610-14, of Emperor Jahengir receiving his son, Prince Parvis, in *durbar* gives a vivid picture of court ceremonial.

at Amritsar. Built on old foundations, it was started in 1764 but not finished and gilded until the early nineteenth century.

The Mughal emperors enthusiastically supported art. Less orthodox than the earlier Moslem rulers of India, they encouraged rather than banned human and animal figures in art. Under the patronage of emperors like Akbar (ruled 1556–1605) Persian, central Asian and Indian painters developed a distinct Mughal style of painting. But European influences also crept into Mughal style, such as the halo, and sunset and cloud effects. Many miniatures were painted by more than one man.

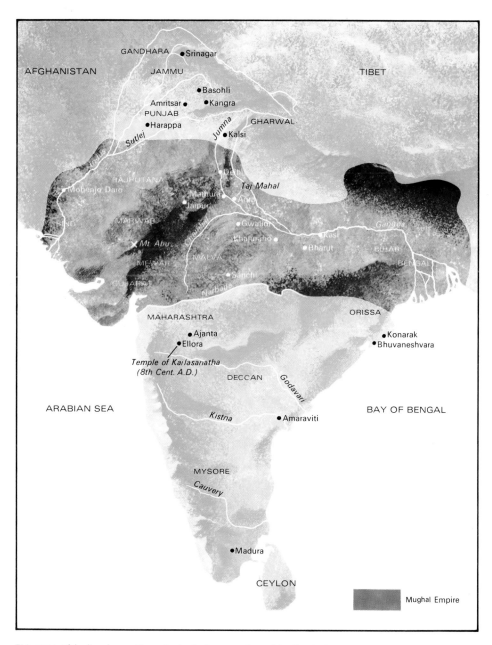

This map of India shows the principal sites mentioned in the text.

13

The young woman in *The Swing*, c. 1810, is typical of the Kangra school. The swing, an old Indian theme, symbolizes love menaced by threatening clouds.

women's passionate desires. Peacocks perch on the lonely beds of fretting beauties while lightning flashes across the black sky; near-demented women brave snakes and goblins to journey through primeval jungles in search of their lovers.

By about the end of the nineteenth century the creativeness of the Mughal-Rajput schools of painting was exhausted. India's rulers thrust English education and European taste upon Indian intellectuals and artists, who consequently turned to Europe for inspiration and example. The Indo-European style that emerged in the early twentieth century was not of great merit. More recently, Indian artists have attempted to reconcile current artistic fashions of the Western world with their own deep-rooted tradition, rather than copying either, and evolve a more harmonious blend of styles.

Quiet artists of a stormy land

Delicate, crackled glaze on a fragile vase; remote, pale landscapes of mountain and sea - a sense of eternity has lingered in the art of China for 3,500 years of turbulent history.

CHINA HAS a continuous artistic tradition extending over 3,500 years. Generally, her art is quiet and conservative rather than exotic, reflecting the continuity of Chinese culture and the influence of Confucianism. On the other hand Taoist influences run like a thread through almost the whole of Chinese art, making for simplicity and the striving for mystic union with nature.

While much Chinese painting and sculpture is Buddhist, the Indian philosophy-religion of Buddhism has never quite penetrated the soul of Chinese culture to the same depth as Confucianism and Taoism. Nevertheless, Buddhism caught the imagination of many Chinese artists because it provided a vehicle for the expression of popular religious feeling beyond the scope of Taoism and Confucianism. Other foreign influences, especially ideas from western and central Asia, were also assimilated into Chinese culture. In principle, the aim of Chinese artists has always been to project ideas and feelings in addition to aesthetically pleasing visual representations.

Traditional Chinese architecture is picturesque, and the serene statues of the Buddha impressive, but neither architecture nor sculpture represents the best in Chinese art. Chinese ivory and lacquer work is of outstanding beauty. The Chinese have always prized jade, which for them symbolized charity, integrity, wisdom, courage and similar virtues. Exquisite silks were produced in China 2,000 years before any other country understood the technique of silk production. Traders carried the silks across Asia to the Mediterranean for sale to wealthy pur-

Chinese Dynasties

Shang-Yin	1523–1027 BC
Chou	1027–221
Warring States	480–221
Ch'in	221–206
Han	BC 206–220 AD
Three Kingdoms	220–265
Six Dynasties	265–588
Sui	589–618
T'ang	618–906
Five Dynasties	906–959
Sung	960–1279
Yüan	1280–1368
Ming	1368–1644
Ch'ing	1644–1912
Republic	1912–

chasers in ancient Rome. In China, rich courtiers wore brilliantly dyed silk costumes decorated with swastikas and dragons, birds, insects, flowers, and many more intricate designs.

Until the thirteenth century, Chinese artists painted their pictures on silk because this was the most durable and suitable material available. After this time, most painters began to use paper, although some still preferred to paint on silk.

Except for small paintings in books, almost all Chinese paintings are in the form of scrolls, with wooden rods at the ends. Some hang vertically, some horizontally. Many painters have used long, horizontal scrolls to paint riverside scenery. When the scroll is unrolled it is as though the viewer is in a moving boat watching the shore: scene follows scene, with calligraphic explanation in between. Calligraphy and painting are closely related in Chinese art, and the same kind of brushwork is used for both.

This highly elaborate bronze vessel is in the shape of an owl and is mounted on three legs. It was produced during the Shang-Yin dynasty.

A Chinese artist is necessarily a calligrapher before he is a painter.

Gifts for the gods

Many bronze containers, mounted on three supporting legs, were produced by unknown craftsmen between the beginning of the Shang-Yin dynasty and the end of the Han dynasty (c. 1500 BC to AD 220). These vessels usually held food and wine offered to the gods in ancestor-worship ceremonies, but some rich families used them as domestic utensils. The vessels also had ceremonial significance and conferred status upon those who possessed them. The vessels vary in height from a few inches to about four feet, and in weight from a few ounces to about 1,500 pounds. Some are plain, some have symbolic, highly stylized, geometrical patterns. Others are highly decorated with human figures or animals, birds, reptiles and insect motifs. Some depict scenes of sacrifice, hunting, war or happenings in daily life. About 1,000 of these superb pieces have been found, and together they give a great insight into the life of ancient China.

Early Chinese buildings were made of wood and packed earth, with stone bases for pillars. Recent excavations have unearthed the remains of several large buildings, one of them more than 90 feet long. The early houses had gables and overhanging roofs. Written records reveal that ancient China had well-planned cities, with temples and royal palaces. Ballads tell of elaborate porches, gates and courtyards. Nearly 2,500 years ago, Confucius complained that buildings had already become too decorative. Most traditional buildings extended horizontally rather than vertically. When tall buildings were constructed, they were so designed that they swayed with the wind; they were topped with sloping roofs which reduced the impact of the wind.

Apart from the written records, much of present knowledge about ancient Chinese architecture comes from clay models of buildings, and reliefs on tiles and stone slabs. Archaeologists found these objects, together with delightful models of ox carts, wells, stables and granaries, buried in tombs dating from the period of the Han dynasty (206 BC–AD 220).

By about the first century AD, motifs from southwestern Asia and the eastern Mediterranean made their way into China. Sculptors began to produce fabulous winged lions and winged and fierce horned dragon-headed creatures to guard the tombs of Chinese emperors. Tomb wall-paintings from about the same period show lively scenes of guests arriving on horse-back or by chariot at friendly gatherings, to be entertained by musicians.

From the fourth century AD onwards, Chinese Buddhists cut cave temples and giant images of the Buddha from the rock face in Indian fashion. At the 'Caves of the Thousand Buddhas', at Tun-huang in Kansu, more than 400 grottoes were carved out from the cliff. Chinese Buddhists also developed a style of sculpture that took inspiration from the *Mathura* and *Gandhara* styles of India. But their art, like their religion, became less and less Indian with the passing of time.

Buddhas in elaborate shrines

The rhythmical movement of Indian figures disappeared. The body became less important, the face more so. The Buddha's image became less aesthetically exciting, more impressive and serene. Chinese sculptors designed their Buddhas to be viewed from the front only; the back of most of their figures has little interest.

Early Buddhist images were set up in shrines which gradually became more and more elaborate. Wooden temples and monasteries became as grand as palaces, with galleries, pavilions, courtyards and gardens. *Stupas* (domed monuments built in India to house sacred Buddhist relics) caught the imagination of Chinese Buddh-

ists returning from pilgrimages to India. The Chinese already possessed multi-storey wooden buildings and these gradually evolved into the Chinese counterpart of the stupa, the *pagoda*. The earliest surviving Chinese pagoda, a 12-sided stone tower built in AD 520 in Honan, shows Indian influence. But later, pagodas became more traditionally Chinese in style. Most Chinese pagodas have between

The earliest surviving Chinese pagoda, a 12-sided stone tower in Honan, dates back to AD 520. This form of architecture developed from the Indian *stupa*, which housed sacred Buddhist relics.

Dappled green glaze covers this pottery lion, made during the T'ang dynasty, a period notable for the advance in the art of ceramics.

with the subject matter, carefully plan space and composition, and imitate early paintings of high quality. These six principles have guided Chinese painters since Hsieh Ho's time. They are not dissimilar from guidelines laid down for judging paintings by a secretary of the French Academy in 1680.

During the T'ang dynasty (618–906) China came into increasingly close trading contact with the outside world. Mosques and even Christian churches were built in Ch'ang-an, the T'ang capital. Foreign

A lady of the T'ang period, made of fired terracotta, of the type which often accompanied the dead to their tombs as companions in the after life.

five and 12 storeys.

One of the earliest known Chinese artists was Ku K'ai-Chih, a calligrapher-painter and poet who lived in the fourth century A D. Wild, unconventional and witty, he was a favourite at court. He painted portraits of courtiers, using Taoist-inspired landscapes as incidental background. It is said that he captured not only the likeness of his sitters, but also the essence of their spirit. Between c. A D 300 and 600, many Buddhist paintings appeared.

In c. A D 500, Hsieh Ho, a portrait painter of Nanking, set forth six principles of painting which gave technical and aesthetic guidance to painters and art critics. Hsieh Ho laid down that the painter should cause the breath of vitality to flow through a painting, make firm bone-like strokes and give form and shape to his work. He should use colours in harmony

Since ancient times, jade has been prized by the Chinese. For its qualities of strength, purity and colour, the Han scholar Hsü Shen endowed it with five virtues: charity, rectitude, wisdom, courage and equity. This little horse was probably carved during the T'ang dynasty.

cultural influences were assimilated and these enriched Chinese art. T'ang craftsmanship ranged from imaginative filigree work to ornate sarcophagi, from finely carved ivories to masterpieces of metalwork in gold, silver and bronze. Chinese painters caught the spirit of affluence and optimism which surrounded them. They painted plump, stately women of the T'ang court grouped together to pursue respectable domestic activities such as silkmaking or, perhaps, more frivolously, to while away their time playing games.

In the eighth century, a dynamic school of Buddhist painting emerged under the leadership of Wu Tao-Tzu. His temple murals revealed ecstatic visions of gods and goddesses in paradise, with a touch of Indian sensuality and rhythm. No bigot, Wu Tao-Tzu also painted portraits of Confucius and Lao Tzu (the traditional founder of Taoism). All his paintings were later destroyed in a great purge of the Buddhists in 843, but other artists imitated his work.

Between the end of the T'ang dynasty and the end of the Sung (960–1279), artists developed 'mountain and water' landscapes on Buddhist-Taoist themes. They painted saints, sages and immortals meditating in remote hermitages on inaccessible mountains. Colour, shape and space were meticulously arranged. A mood of peaceful simplicity pervades their works, which have a deep mystical significance.

A detail from a silk scroll painted by Hui-tsung, a gifted emperor of the Sung dynasty, shows court ladies ironing silk.

Chinese porcelain led the world in its beauty of shape and colour during the Sung dynasty and many varieties were produced. *Celadon* ware, much prized outside China, was the colour of leaf or bluish green. Nervous Arab rulers liked to possess it because they believed that it cracked, or changed colour, if brought into contact with poison. *Lung-Ch'üan* ware was light grey, but burnt yellowish when fired in the kiln. *Crackle* (cracking which occurs in firing because the glaze shrinks more than the body) came to be prized for its decorative effect, and was often deliberately induced. A finer, secondary crackle was developed too.

Disaster came to China in 1279 when the Mongols swept down from the north and established the Yüan dynasty in Peking. Many Chinese scholars fled the court and retired into seclusion to devote their days to painting and literature. In isolation, the painters tended to develop individual styles – a new development in China's conservative art. Their broad aesthetic interests led to a closer relationship between poetry, calligraphy and painting. Some scholar-artists, using delicate brush strokes, incorporated their poems into their paintings.

Gentlemen-artists continued to paint during the time of the Ming dynasty, which replaced Mongol rule in 1368. Their artistic interest spread to architecture, garden design and art collecting. Professional painters at the Ming court, however, were forced to observe academic rules that inhibited the creativeness of their works. They sought to compensate for this by using brilliant colours and creating decorative forms.

Porcelain and jade

During the Ming dynasty porcelain became much more colourful. The Ming 'blue and white' (glazed porcelain with blue decoration), imitated in Japan, Persia and southeastern Asia, inspired the porcelain of Delf. The Chinese produced vast quantities of Ming porcelain, much

Love of colour and luxury characterized the Ming dynasty: blue and white ware produced during it, like this beautifully decorated flask, has been admired and imitated in many different countries. Below, a camel carved in limestone, one of 12 animals which line the Sacred Way to the tomb of Ming Emperor Yung-lo.

of which they exported. In 1643, nearly 130,000 pieces of porcelain, mostly from one manufacturing centre, were shipped to the Netherlands alone. Jade lost its ritual significance, but was increasingly valued for its pleasing appearance, and jade work reached a high peak of craftsmanship.

In 1644, the Chinese Ming dynasty fell, to be replaced by the Ch'ing (Manchurian) dynasty, which lasted until 1912. Again, artists fled from the foreign court; some retired, some became monks. The Ch'ing emperors valued Chinese culture and pursued conservative policies in order to preserve it. Some of the emperors themselves became artists. The dilettante emperor Ch'ien-lung (reigned 1736–96) built

To escape the oppressive atmosphere of the Ming court, poets, painters and calligraphers flocked to the south. Shen Chou was an influential artist of the Wu school. In *Landscape* we see his feeling of communion with nature expressed in a stylized manner with very individual brushwork.

up a vast art collection. Eight thousand of his paintings survive in the Palace Museum of Formosa. He invited an Italian Jesuit, Joseph Castiglione (an accomplished artist) to his court, who took the title and name Privy Councillor Lang Shih-ning. Through Castiglione, characteristics of European painting, such as perspective and shading, came into Chinese art. But the artist-emperor ruled that these characteristics were interesting as craftsmanship rather than true art, and Castiglione's influence did not last. Most painters in Ch'ing times took inspiration from the past and tried to interpret and re-create the styles of old masters. They cared little for their subject matter, but placed great emphasis on techniques.

The Ch'ing emperors patronized the ceramics industry, and their officials took a hand in its management. Vast quantities of Ch'ing porcelain were produced in

During the next dynasty, the Ch'ing, the production of porcelain in the Imperial factories attained new heights of perfection; this vase depicts a scene from everyday life.

22

Good-luck symbols carved in red lacquer decorate this wooden throne of the Ch'ing dynasty, which stood before the gate of Ch'ien-lung's hunting palace in Peking.

Of the same period is this tapestry showing one of the mythical monsters of China.

Left, the Summer Palace Pai Yun Tien was built outside Peking by the Dowager Empress Tzu-hsi of the Ch'ing dynasty. She used the money raised for the purpose of forming a navy, and was much condemned for her extravagance.

brilliant colours. Simple designs, often of flowers and birds, decorated early Ch'ing porcelain. Later, these were replaced by landscapes, scenes from everyday life, or illustrations to stories. Ch'ing lacquer work was also produced in factories controlled by the emperors. Lacquered wood chests and cupboards, often inlaid with jade, mother-of-pearl, or semi-precious stones, became highly popular among wealthy Europeans.

Painting in present-day China is either in traditional style, full of vitality and originality, or is Western-inspired.

The art of Japan

Expert borrowers, the artists and craftsmen of Japan transformed China's art forms into a distinctive style of their own. Silk, swords and ceramics were among the media they worked with skill.

ALL JAPANESE arts and crafts are related to each other, and all are intricately bound up with the national religion of Shinto, or with Buddhism, which entered Japan from China in about the sixth century A D. Japan's artists have always stressed the importance of design and had a lively appreciation of colour and an eye for dramatic aspects of the passing scene.

Practically the whole of Japanese art derives at least partly from Chinese or Korean culture. The exceptions to the general rule are the earliest Japanese sculpture, which may be national in inspiration, and the later art, much of which incorporates Western ideas and techniques. But although so much of Japan's culture was borrowed, Japanese artists revitalized what they took, trans-muting it into new, essentially Japanese forms. An intense feeling for nature – the essence of Shinto – permeates all Japan's art.

The characteristic expression of Japanese art is through painting and prints, executed almost exclusively in water-colours or ink. Other important forms of art include architecture, sculpture, ceramics, textiles, lacquer-work and metalwork. Swords, kimonos, theatre and temple masks, dress fasteners and tomb posts have all been developed into highly complex art forms by the Japanese.

The oldest surviving Japanese works of art are crude but impressive clay figures sculpted in the middle or late *Jomon* (rope-pattern) period, between *c.* 3000 B C and 100 B C. These bizarre, barely human figures were probably first made as fertility symbols. Many represent pregnant women, and it is likely that men in ancient Japan prayed to them, begging that their wives might have many sons. The figures vary between about two and 12 inches in height. The earliest of them were crudely

Key Periods in Japanese Art

Prehistoric ... ...until A D	552
(Jomon and Yayoi)	
Asuka ... ...A D	552–646
Nara	710–794
Heian	794–1185
Kamakura	1185–1392
Muromachi	1378–1573
Moyama	1573–1615
Edo or Tokugawa	1615–1867

eyes, which give them a piercing, ghost-like intensity. The Haniwa figures are essentially Japanese, but the funerary purpose for which they were used suggests that even at this early stage Japan was influenced by the culture of China, which dominated Japanese art until very recent times. There is a Japanese legend, however, that Haniwa figures were originally made as life-saving substitutes for royal servants, and were used in a modification of the custom that when an emperor or empress died the servants were buried alive with their royal master or mistress, to wait on them for ever.

When Buddhism came to Japan from China in the sixth century A D, it complemented the native religion of Shinto, rather than replaced it. Along with Buddhist missionaries came Chinese and Korean craftsmen who taught the Japanese new forms and techniques.

Left, a clay figure from the neolithic Jomon period, probably made as a fertility symbol. A crude attempt at decoration was made by pressing straw against the wet clay. *Below*, this ghost-like *Haniwa* sculpture was one of the many human and animal figures erected in circles round burial mounds in the Yayoi period.

decorated, perhaps by pressing straw or matting against the wet clay. Most of these figures were probably the private property of hunters and fisher-folk of Stone-Age Japan. It is likely that their owners hung them from the tent-like roofs of their houses, which were no more than holes dug in the ground.

A new pattern of sculpture, *Haniwa* (circle of clay) figures, flourished during the third and fourth centuries A D. The more interesting Haniwa figures represent people, animals, houses, furniture and personal possessions. These clay figures are so named because they were set in concentric circles in burial mounds. Craftsmen made them hastily on the death of important people. The figures are hollow and stand between 20 and 40 inches high. They have holes and slits for mouth and

Japanese sculptors began to work in wood, clay lacquer, dry lacquer and bronze, producing mostly statues of the Buddha or his disciples. Always quick to learn new techniques, the Japanese produced some of the best Buddhist sculpture.

While the Chinese usually regarded sculptors as merely craftsmen, the Japanese honoured them as artists. *Ateliers* (artists' studios) grew up, where outstanding sculptors supervised their students. Images were made in separate parts, and assembled by the students for completion by the master.

Although most Japanese sculpture is Buddhist, a powerful portrait sculpture, based on the Shinto religion, flourished during the period of the Kamakura *shoguns,* or military commanders (1185–1333). Generally, however, Japanese sculpture began to decline from the twelfth century.

In architecture, the coming of Chinese culture into Japan brought a fairly advanced style of temple construction. Horyuji Temple, near Nara, is the best preserved example. It was built on the beam and pillar principle, and has screening walls that are non-structural. Like all traditional Japanese building it was con-

Free from Chinese influence is this fine lacquer cosmetic box of the Heian period, inlaid with mother-of-pearl on a gold, silver and black background.

Robes with flowing sleeves decorated in red, dark blue and cream lacquer adorn this wooden figure of a Shinto deity (Kamakura period).

27

Not only the oldest temple in Japan, but the oldest wooden building in the world, Horyuji Temple was built in the Asuka period by Prince Shotoku.

structed mainly of wood. Horyuji was first built in about AD 607 and reconstructed in about 700, by which time more than 500 Buddhist shrines, monasteries and temples had been built. Horyuji Temple is believed to be the world's oldest existing wooden building. Although temples built after Horyuji were bigger and more elaborate, they were constructed on the same basic principles.

In ancient Japan, the capital city changed whenever an emperor died, because it was thought that his death polluted the area of the court. One such

change occurred in 710 when the new city of Nara, built in the Chinese style, became the capital. This occurred at about the time Horyuji Temple was rebuilt. It was followed by a great burst of architectural activity. As part of the general Chinese cultural influence of the time, the most typical shape of pagoda was introduced into Japan.

From 794, religious architecture ceased to dominate, and *Shindenzukuri* (the architectural style of the nobility) came into being. After about 1185, architecture became less Chinese in style. Simpler houses were built for the warrior class. Shelves and niches were added to the normally plain interiors of houses, so that paintings and other works of art could be conveniently displayed. The elaborate tea ceremony – an art in itself – became popular and also influenced the design of house interiors. Other characteristics of Japanese architecture introduced about this time were *tokonoma* (alcoves) and *shoji* (sliding paper doors).

During the Kamakura period, Japanese craftsmen developed ceramic ware, following the superb example of China under the Sung dynasty (ended 1279). Japanese porcelain has never equalled that of China in quality, but it has infinitely more variety. In the seventeenth century, Japanese potters produced many beautiful works of porcelain, their special achievement being coloured, treacly glazes. Much of this porcelain was produced for the tea ceremony.

The oldest existing Japanese paintings, dating from the sixth century, are Buddhist wall-paintings and scrolls in the Chinese style. Zen Buddhist black and white ink sketches, simply but skilfully drawn, were also based on Chinese forms, and these became very popular. In time, however, the themes that painters chose became

A golden pavilion built to gratify the taste of Yoshimitsu, a shogun (military commander) of the Muromachi period, graces a delightful garden in Kyoto. Later it was converted into a Zen Buddhist temple.

more and more secular.

Painting reached a high peak during the Kamakura period when, having absorbed Chinese tradition, artists struck new, essentially Japanese styles. At this time there were close links between the visual arts and literature. Rich, varied and colourful scroll-paintings on silk, called *e-makimono,* gave visual representations of literary themes. Most of these scrolls were painted between 898 and 1333.

Strip cartoons

At first illustrations were provided to accompany the text, or the artist displayed his calligraphic skill with delicately written captions to the pictures. Later the full flowering of scroll technique led to the total elimination of the written word. As the scroll was unrolled, so was the story, vivid scenes succeeding one another so that the viewer could 'read' them as clearly as a book. This was probably the most sophisticated and charming

1 A delicate tracery of branches and flowers in gold enamel decorates this vase of the early Edo period, which is purely Japanese in style. **2** Travellers from the West inspired tremendous interest after the arrival of the Jesuits in 1542.

This early Edo screen of the type known as *Namban Byobu* ('screens of the southern barbarians') depicts Portuguese merchants disembarking bearing strange wares from overseas.

form of what we know today as the strip-cartoon technique. But while the modern cartoon artist bases his technique on simple drawing and the elimination of detail, the scroll artists of the Kamakura period revelled in exquisite little pictures, rich in colour and imagery, with the whole range of emotions – humour, violence, sympathy and at times a cruel caricature – entrancing and absorbing the viewer.

In Japan, art has always tended to impinge on the more mundane areas of life. Objects which in other countries have been manufactured merely for their utility, have given Japanese craftsmen scope to develop their artistry. In particular they have excelled in *tsuba* (sword-guards) and *inro* and *netsuke* (men's dress accoutrements). Exquisite craftwork in a variety of forms was produced during the Tokugawa period (1603–1867).

Japanese craftsmen took a delight in swords and sword furniture generally, particularly tsuba, some of which were as delicately made as jewellery. Aristocrats often exchanged tsuba as gifts, and many were never actually fitted to sword blades.

Inro were small ornamental flat lacquer-work cases, which men hung from the sashes of their kimonos by silken cords. The word *inro* means seal-containers, and they were originally worn to contain the personal seals of the wearer, ready for use. Later, inro made with several compartments were used to contain things which a Western-clad man might carry in his pockets – medicines, sweets and tobacco, for example. (Both men and women took to smoking when the Portuguese introduced the habit in the sixteenth century.) Inro were attached to the sash by *netsuke* – miniature works of art intricately carved in wood, bamboo, ivory, bone or horn, or wrought in metal. Netsuke took a variety of forms; rats, wrestlers, gods, demons, lucky charms, masks – all these served as subjects for the craftsman's art. Painters, swordmakers, woodcarvers and other

Sword guards like these, complete with fierce warriors and animals, were often exchanged as gifts by rich aristocrats.

artist-craftsmen found the making of netsuke figures a profitable sideline. Some craftsmen achieved marvellous results, carving, for example, 24 Chinese stories inside a two-inch-high netsuke in the shape of a bamboo shoot.

'Unsurpassed under heaven'

Each form of Japanese art tends to impinge upon other forms, giving the arts a cohesive quality. As literature provided themes for the scroll-paintings, so the theatre provided scope for the development of mask-making into a form of art. Several stylized masks were worn by performers in each Nō play (a highly conventionalized combination of dancing, chanting and music). Nō plays reached their peak in the fifteenth century. The masks expressed various emotions: kindness, cruelty, love, fury, passion, idiocy and so on. Mask-making became the specialized craft of a number of families, who passed the profession on from father to son, claiming that their work was 'unsurpassed under heaven'. Masks were also used in other forms of theatre such as *kyogen* (comic interludes in Kabuki drama)

The Japanese were superb craftsmen and lavished their artistry on the most prosaic objects. A man carried this *inro* (seal container), *left,* attached to his sash by an intricately carved *netsuke, right,* in the shape of a lion. Art reached the ordinary people with the adoption of the colour print from China in the eighteenth century.

and *kagura* (Shinto shrine and temple dances).

The idea of the colour print also came from China, but Japanese artists gave it an entirely new form. Between 1740 and 1890 they developed it into a vigorous and popular art that portrayed everyday life, the theatre, geishas and courtesans, and also the make-believe world of monsters and ghosts. Vast numbers of prints were stamped from blocks and sold cheaply; for the first time art was identified with the

common people rather than with the court and the privileged classes. The sedate, respectable works of the scroll painters gave way to the energetic, intensely alive art of the masses. Despised by the traditional patrons of art, the colour prints were at first produced to illustrate the new popular literature read by the rising commercial classes. Later, they were eagerly bought to decorate the walls of even the humblest houses. Many of the prints were of the kind called *ukiyo-ye* (pictures of the passing scene).

The early prints were stamped in black from heavy wood blocks, which were cut away so that the lines stood out in relief. In time, colour was added. The black and white proofs were hand-painted, and later several blocks were used to give multi-coloured prints.

Hishikawa Moronobu (1625–1694)

largely began the new art, producing lively woodcuts for book illustrations. Many of his prints show stockily built women, often in compromising situations. Hishikawa Moronobu's pupil, Torii Kiyonobu (1664–1729) and his son Torii Kiyomasu (1706–63), developed the public's craze for dramatic prints of actors, and produced posters for the Kabuki theatre. These prints and posters remained popular until the end of the nineteenth century.

Okumura Masanobu (1685–1764) portrayed pretty but rather chubby girls in long kimonos, adding pink and green to the black of earlier prints. Suzuki Harunobu (1725–70), however, was probably the originator of the polychrome print, which had as many as ten colours. His female figures were slimmer, more delicate than those of earlier print artists. He grouped them in the interesting settings of the world they lived in.

The print artist who really painted women to the greatest degree of elegance was Kitagawa Utamaro (1753–1806). He drew inspiration for his work by living in the *Yoshiwara* – the courtesans' sector of Edo (present-day Tokyo). Kitagawa Utamaro tended to idealize his women, but he also set them against realistic backgrounds, portraying them surrounded by admiring customers.

A prolific eccentric

During the year 1794–5 Toshusai Sharuku, who may once have been an actor himself, produced prints caricaturing actors, showing them often masked, playing women's parts in plays. The starkness of his prints offended the public, who resented having

One of the *Thirty-six Views of Fuji,* by Hokusai Katsushika, who influenced Gauguin and Van Gogh.

One of the *Fifty-three Stations of the Tokaido Road* by Hiroshige Ando.

their favourite actors parodied, and in his lifetime Toshusai Sharuku's works remained unsold.

One of the most prolific, dedicated and eccentric artists of all time, Hokusai Katsushika (1760–1849) is believed to have produced more than 30,000 prints, before his frenzied and unhappy life came to an end at the age of nearly 90. His prints, which influenced Paul Gauguin, Vincent van Gogh, and other European painters, concentrated on nature and superb landscapes. His works include *Thirty-six Views of Fuji, A Hundred Views of Fuji* and *Famous Bridges and Waterfalls.* Hiroshige Ando (1797–1858) was a master of landscapes, whose prints influenced James McNeill Whistler. They include *Fifty-three Stations of the Tokaido Road,* and *A Hundred Views of Edo.*

Western influences, which first penetrated Japan in the late sixteenth century, were almost entirely excluded by the government in the mid-seventeenth. Western ideas again entered Japan after 1868, with unhappy effects on the arts. The Japanese are currently developing new styles, achieving a more harmonious blending of eastern and western inspiration.

Magic and ritual shape Africa's art

Joy in life suffuses the art of Africa, affirming supernatural powers and the energy of human existence. Here these ancient cultures are enshrined, their meaning and their wisdom recorded.

UNTIL QUITE RECENTLY, it was fashionable among scholars to exclude pre-colonial Africa south of the Sahara from the study of world history. No written records existed, missionary-explorers returned with accounts of primitive and pagan practices, and their reports of social chaos – resulting largely from the disruptive slave trade – all contributed to a basic misconception. It seemed an inescapable conclusion that the desert wastes of the Sahara had sealed off Africa in historical times, and that in their isolation the Negro peoples had achieved no culture nor created any civilization. African tribal art, which lacked the true proportions of idealized classical European art, seemed crude and barbaric.

Despite the lack of written records, however, African myths and legends contain marvellous stories of past glories. The chronicles of Arab travellers in the Middle Ages give exotic descriptions of empires and kingdoms in western Africa that had all the glory and splendour of the *Arabian Nights*. From these chronicles, from the myths and from the pioneering work of archaeologists, the broad history of the rise and fall of the great West African empires has been pieced together.

Spiritual depth

The emergence of Cubism and other twentieth-century abstract art in Europe was partly inspired by African work. These art styles have helped us to appreciate African culture. We see that the distortions in African art were not evidence of the primitive and the unsophisticated, but were purposeful and part of a profoundly religious and philosophical tradition.

The sculpture of western Africa, forming the pinnacle of sub-Saharan art, covers a wide variety of forms from naturalism to abstraction, but the finest work reflects a sublime serenity, a spiritual depth and a dynamic force that stem from African tribal religion. The disregard for naturalism in much of African art, and the distorted representation of the human body, arise from the artist's belief in a 'vital force' or energy coming from God, and filling the universe and all living

1

things. This force is the centre of all thought and action.

The agricultural peoples of western Africa had such highly advanced and deeply felt religious and philosophical beliefs that, first Moslem and later, Christian missionaries found it extremely difficult to implant new ideas and root out the old. Most of the Bantu-speaking peoples of western Africa and the Lower Congo region believed in one God who is all-powerful. Because God permeates the whole world, the Africans felt no need to worship him, and did not try to represent him in their art. Their worship was devoted to their ancestors, the most important being those first created by God, whose spirits were asked to intercede with God on their behalf. Artists made statues of ancestors which, if occupied by a spirit, became objects of great power, to which the farmer could address his request for a good harvest, or the barren woman her plea for children. Such statues were often adorned, sacrifices were made to them and offerings such as fresh beer and meat were placed before them.

Some artists believed that the more beautiful the statue representing an ancestor, the more likely the spirit was to occupy it. African sculptors did not strive for beauty in the European sense – their art was functional. They were trying to capture an effect which would serve a religious purpose. They concentrated, therefore, on investing their work with the highest degree of spiritual significance; anything not essential to this purpose was excluded. The positions of the human figures are also related to their religious function. Many ancestor statues are seated

in a state of repose, and are probably represented as living chiefs. A statue of an ancestor represents an attempt to make the invisible spirit visible.

Because of their belief in universal

1 Ancestor figures were worshipped for their power to intercede with God the Creator. Belief in life after death is found all over Africa. This effigy of an ancestor, of wood covered with beaten brass, is from the Congo. 2 A calabash (gourd), surmounted by a bird, served to hold bones of ancestors.

energy, it was not surprising that fertility was a vital aspect of the Africans' thought.

Carved female figures represent devotees of the goddess of plenty and well-being.

Mother and child figures are examples of fertility. Further, breasts out of all proportion to the rest of the body, accentuated navels and swollen abdomens were common features of African statuary. The head was also, for our taste, generally too large for the body: because it was the seat of thought, the artist exaggerated it to show its true significance. The very material used by the artist reflected his belief in the vital force. Carving from wood, the commonest material, invested in the statue the power of the living tree. Cutting the wood often became a ritual in which the artist begged the tree's forgiveness for harming it.

Although the human figure had special religious meaning, carvings of animals were important too. Animals also possessed the vital force, and the mythical ancestors of the tribe often appear as animals. Statues and other representations of animals were often stylized to convey the character of the animal: elephants and buffaloes represented strength; leopards implied ferocity; snakes were often the symbol for life and eternity; and tortoises suggested old age. Sometimes human and animal forms were combined in one figure, heightening the meaning of the object.

Many African tribes held the traditional artist in awe or even fear, regarding him as a magician or witch-doctor. Ritual and magic have a major bearing on African art. Some tribes used large, often fearsome, masks in ritual ceremonies. The masks, the forms of which had a considerable effect on the work of such European artists as Pablo Picasso and Amedeo Modigliani, represented examples of dynamic art, as opposed to the static quality of the statues.

One of the most important rituals in African life was the initiation or circumcision ceremony, through which children passed from childhood to adulthood. Masks were often used in these rites, some

Rich in mythology, the African peoples commemorated their beliefs in their art. On this carved and painted wooden bowl of the Yoruba in Nigeria, the python, symbol of life, curves protectingly over the man and woman, on whose union life depends.

body. Sometimes fetishes were used to harm enemies. Perhaps because of hypnosis or auto-suggestion, such magic, even today, often seems extraordinarily effective. However, most fetishes were thrown away after use.

Magic permeated African art, and was even evident in rock paintings, the earliest known art in sub-Saharan Africa. On the walls of caves, the artists tried to establish a magical union between the painting and the object portrayed. Paintings often referred to hunting expeditions, war, fertility rites or the need for rain.

Such art can only survive as long as the beliefs on which it is based survive. Today,

Ritual and magic are deeply involved in African art. Masks were used in all kinds of ceremonies, in ritual dances to deliver people possessed of demons, in rites of the dead or in the important ceremonies for initiating children into the secrets of adulthood, like this one from he Bayaka of the Congo.

of which represented symbolically a state of childhood and were removed when the initiation rites were concluded. Masks were worn in ritual dances to deliver people possessed by demons. In rites of the dead, some tribes used white masks, the colour being associated with ghosts and spirits. Masks were also used by secret societies.

Fetishes and rock paintings

Magic was part of the religion of the Bantu-speaking peoples of eastern and southern Africa. The African saw the universe as a sea of forces imparting energy and he attempted to harness these forces to strengthen his own vital force. Witch-doctors made fetishes, objects that were consecrated for such purposes as protecting people against illness and misfortune. Some fetishes were crude models of people with nails driven all over the truly traditional religious art is produced in only a few areas, and the tourist who collects souvenirs is unlikely to come across it. But where it does survive, this art offers striking proof of the continuity of art forms and styles. Anthropologists have discovered work made recently that is practically identical with work done a hundred years ago. The abstractions and unusual forms that characterize much of African art are the result of tradition, and represent the vision of a particular tribe or group, not of an individual artist though an individual's style is often evident.

The work of modern African artists, who are influenced by European styles, does not have a religious origin, and neither did the work of some earlier artists. The well-known Benin bronzes, many of which illustrate military themes, were made for decorative purposes under the patronage of the *Obas,* the god-like kings of Benin, in what is now south-central Nigeria. Work associated with other royal courts, such as Ashanti, Bakuba and Dahomey, served a similar decorative and generally non-religious function.

A finely worked gold badge from Ashanti in Ghana, worn by 'soulwashers' who shielded the king's soul from evil.

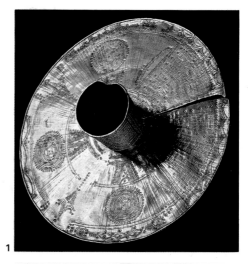

1

2

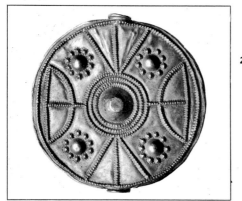

1 Suffering for the sake of elegance, the Ibo women of eastern Nigeria wore these gold anklets from adolescence onwards. 2 Man and woman, the life-giving force, face each other with arms entwined on this finely carved wooden head-rest made by the Luba of the Congo region.

The art of the people of sub-Saharan Africa is expressed in many ways. Apart from the religious statues and masks, some tribes have constructed elegant buildings, decorated with paintings in geometric designs. Many homes are adorned by finely woven baskets and mats, as well as elegant domestic implements. Often the abstract patterns on such domestic products have considerable symbolic meaning. Pastoral tribes in some areas also produce fine leatherwork from the hides of their cattle. Towering above all other artistic achievements, however, is sculpture, which occurs most frequently in western Africa, especially Nigeria, and in the Congo Basin.

The most popular material used in sculpture is wood. Unfortunately, in a humid climate wooden objects have a short life, and their decay is generally completed by ants. For this reason few wooden objects of more than about 100 years old have survived. The wood is fashioned by an *adze,* an axe with a transverse blade, combining the functions of mallet and chisel. Fine details are supplied by knives and chisels. On completion, the artist must protect the fresh wood, and he uses several processes, including a coating of soot and grease. Many observers have commented that the tools employed in wood carving are the only primitive aspect of African art, because despite the difficulties of working the results can be incredibly fine.

Clay modelling is also popular, and is used in sculpture throughout West Africa and the Congo Basin. Perhaps the most impressive work was found at the sacred Yoruba city of Ife, in Nigeria, where magnificent terracotta heads were discovered. Terracotta-work was also found at Nok in Nigeria, and is the earliest known African sculpture. But clay objects are generally delicate and easily broken, and as a result, most relics are in fragments. Metal was also found at Nok, and experts consider that iron was probably introduced to Nigeria around 400 B C. The so-called bronzes of western Africa rarely

The Olokun head, discovered at Ife, Nigeria, probably represents a king. Such fine bronze heads, dating back to the thirteenth century, are still being unearthed at this sacred Yoruba city.

An amazing survival from 2,000 years ago, this terracotta head was found at Nok in Nigeria, an example of the earliest known African sculpture.

contain tin, and would be better named *cast brasses*. The main method used in metal casting was the *cire perdue* (lost wax process), whereby a rough clay form was coated with wax, and the detail was modelled upon it. The wax was then covered by another layer of clay, and the molten metal was poured in to replace the wax.

Other materials used by sculptors include ivory and bone. Stone is seldom used. The unusual and mysterious group of 750 stone statues discovered at Esie, a village in Nigeria, are in a poor state. The statues are presumably ancestor figures. The faces of the statues have been largely erased, the result perhaps of many sacrifices when blood was poured over their heads. We know from Arab chronicles that gold was often used at the courts of medieval West African empires, but presumably most of the gold objects were plundered and melted down. An expressive Ashanti mask is one of the few surviving pieces.

Scholars find it almost impossible to trace the historical development of styles and forms in African art, in the way that it is possible to do in Europe. Very little of early African art has yet been discovered. So many of the materials were perishable, so much work was destroyed in war or by zealous missionaries and so many objects were broken up by the members of the tribes themselves once their ritual purpose had been served.

The only historical record – and this is incomplete – has been traced in Nigeria. The earliest sculpture is the terracotta and polished stone which was found at sites of the Nok culture and is dated around 250 B C. The art of Nok was almost certainly not the first flowering of African sculpture, because the heads in particular are surprisingly mature. We know practically nothing about the Nok culture or the centuries that followed before the rise of Ife. From the twelfth to the fourteenth centuries, superb sculpture was made in this sacred city, perhaps the finest yet found in Africa. Historians believe that the artists of Ife must have been influenced by the much earlier Nok culture. The Ife heads and masks in bronze and terracotta are unusually lifelike and are possibly portraits.

The art of Benin

According to tradition, an Ife master visited Benin in the second half of the fourteenth century, and so a connection is established between these two cultures. The Portuguese visited Benin in 1486, and in 1686 a Dutch navigator described the city and its art in glowing terms. The finest Benin art dates from before the seventeenth century; thereafter it becomes stereotyped and imitative.

Among the great variety of bronzes are the heads of Benin rulers, and plaques showing kings waging war. Statuettes of fierce warriors and plaques of hunters have a virile tension. Animals were also used as subjects, particularly the leopard, a sacred beast of Benin. Ivory was used to carve masks and superb leopards. Benin was finally destroyed at the end of the nineteenth century and most of the work is in museums throughout the world. Ife-Benin has attracted world-wide interest in African art, but we must remember that it is court art and differs from tribal religious art in that it is devoted to the secular as well as the religious power of the divine kings. As a result, it is unrepresentative of Nigerian and African art as a whole.

Many difficulties stand in the way of the scholar who tries to classify the thousands of styles represented in African art. The problems of dating have already been mentioned, but in addition styles overlap from group to group and even from village to village. The contrasts between naturalistic, stylized and abstract forms are difficult to establish. All three occur within most groups, and sometimes features of each are contained within one figure.

This friendly animal carved in ivory is a leopard, a sacred beast of Benin. An African fable tells how the leopard got his spots - from a visit by his friend the Fire!

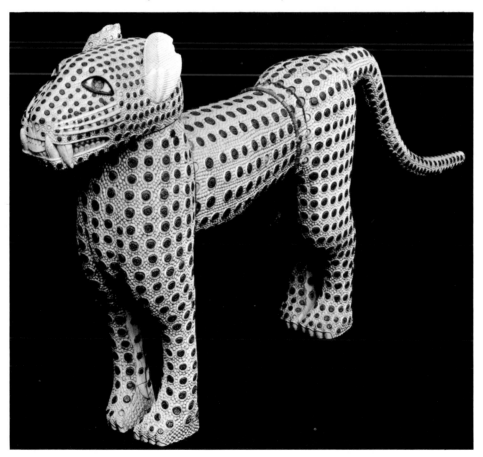

Magnificent bronze- and ivory-work, mostly decorative, was produced in Benin, in south-central Nigeria. A sixteenth-century ivory mask representing the *Oba,* or king, of Benin, is topped with a tiara of miniature heads of Portuguese explorers.

Sub-Saharan African art is sometimes referred to as Negro art to distinguish it from the art of Egypt and northern Africa. But this term implies that tribal art is much more widespread than in fact it is. Further, it is hardly evident in the work of American Negroes.

As we have already seen, tribal art owes its inspiration to deeply held religious and philosophical beliefs. These beliefs have been challenged and eroded for hundreds of years, first by the Moslems and later by the Europeans. The contemporary African artist has been brought up in a world where tribal traditions are breaking down. With justifiable pride in the past, but conscious of the dangers of tribalism in the present, he faces the problem of adapting indigenous African forms to his work.

Art reflects a faith

Many countries contributed to the splendour of the art of Islam. Intimately bound up with a religious faith shared by millions, its supreme expression is in the architecture of the mosques of the Arab world.

ISLAMIC ART is intimately bound up with the spirit of the Islamic religion and it largely centres on the Moslem place of worship, the mosque. It follows that the main form of Islamic art is architecture. The Moslems have hardly any sculpture – a result of the discouragement of image-making by strict Moslems. The Arab tradition of painting came almost to an end early in the eighth century when religious principles began to be more strictly applied. East of the Arab countries, Moslems observed the ban on image-making in religious, but not in secular, art. The Persians perfected a style of miniature-painting, outstanding in beauty of colour and form, which inspired the Mughal and Rajput painters of India.

The art of Islam is a combined product of many countries. Apart from architecture and painting, Moslem artists and craftsmen have applied their talents to carpet- and rug-making, textiles, metalworking, glassware, wood-carving, plasterwork, bookbinding and illustration, and ceramics – particularly tile-making. To a large extent even these arts and crafts have centred round the mosque and its adornment.

Islam came into being when Mohammed fled from Mecca to Medina and was accepted by the Medinans as their leader. This incident, called the *Hegira*, marked the beginning of the Moslem era and coincided with the Christian year AD 622. Mohammed at first prayed to Allah (God) by prostrating himself in the direction of Jerusalem. Later, he turned to face the Kaaba, a pre-Moslem, simply built shrine in Mecca. From that time onwards Moslems have always turned towards Mecca to pray. These happenings had great significance in the development of Islamic architecture.

Churches into mosques

The early Moslems were in spirit tent-dwelling desert nomads, and they had no architecture worthy of the name. When they expanded outside Arabia they took over not only the architectural styles of the peoples they conquered, but also some of their religious buildings. In Syria, for example, which was seized from the Byzantine Empire shortly after Mohammed's death, the Moslems usually converted into mosques one or more of the Christian churches in each captured town. They had no ambition to establish great temples to the glory of God, rather they wanted simple houses of prayer for the faithful.

The conversion of a church into a mosque posed problems. For example, when the Great Church at Hama, in Syria, was converted in 636–7, the Christian congregation, as was normal in churches, looked eastwards to face the altar. But the Moslems had to face south, and to do this they simply converted the western entrances into windows and cut new entrances into the northern wall. Thus they prayed *across* the aisles, facing Mecca. In Persia too, conquered shortly after Syria, the Moslems converted existing buildings into mosques, using impartially Zoroastrian fire temples, or *apadanas* (halls of royal palaces). But in Iraq, where they established new towns, such as Baghdad, they found no suitable buildings and had to construct their own. Their early mosques were extremely simple. At Kufa, for example, they marked out a square, enclosed it by a ditch and built a *zulla* (covered colonnade) along the side nearest to Mecca, using marble from near-by buildings. This, like oasis palms, shielded worshippers from the burning sun.

For a thousand years after Mohammed's time Islam continued to expand. Wherever they went, the Moslems set up mosques, either converting existing buildings or constructing new buildings in a variety of borrowed styles. Yet all their buildings had an architectural unity. A mosque could never be mistaken for any other kind of building. Similarly, when the Moslems came to build *madrasahs* (religious colleges), domed tombs, palaces and other buildings, these bore the characteristic and unmistakable stamp of Islam.

The typical mosque that emerged was basically a rectangular courtyard, called a *haram,* with a fountain or water-basin in the centre, where worshippers could ritually purify themselves before prayer. A colonnade roofed with cupolas often surrounded this courtyard. On the side nearest to Mecca was the house of prayer, almost devoid of furniture, but often richly carpeted. Viewed from the outside, the most distinctive feature of a mosque is its *minarets* (high towers) and it is normally from the top of one of these minarets that the *muezzin* (crier) calls the faithful to prayer five times each day, following the original tradition of Medina. Yet minarets are not essential to the mosque. Many small mosques have no minarets, but most have one or more, four being the most common. Many minarets have a balcony near the top, built to allow the muezzin to cry his message in all directions.

The house of prayer almost always has a domed roof, often onion shaped. This is supported either by solid walls or, more typically, by arcades. Large mosques have interior arcades, part functional, part decorative. Moslem architects used traditional, semicircular arches to carry heavy loads, but evolved new styles of arch for decorative effect, principally horseshoe, four-centred and pointed arches. They created *stalactite* vaulting in which a

Among the arts perfected by the Moslems was that of tile-making. Flowing arabesque, abstract and floral designs adorn the façades of Shakh-i-Zinda, a complex of tombs near Samarkand.

46

number of arch-shaped vaulting cells cover the inner linings of the arches. The decorated arches and stalactite vaulting quickly became typical features of Islamic architecture.

Decorated tiles

The Moslems early developed the craft of glazed tile-making, and many mosque interiors are surfaced with tiles or mosaics of outstanding beauty. Functionally, the tiles have a cooling effect, a useful property, because most mosques are situated in warm or hot climates. The general ban on representations of human or animal figures led Arab artists to experiment with geometrical designs, or to create stylized forms of decoration based on leaves, shoots and tendrils of plants. The cursive Arabic script, intrinsically beautiful, offered another field for experiment. Large plaques often decorate mosque walls and the pillars of internal arcades. These plaques are beautifully inscribed with either the names of Allah, Mohammed, or the first four caliphs, or with quotations from the Koran. The older, rectilinear, form of the Arabic script called *Kufic,* after the city of Kufa in Iraq, was frequently used, and this harmonized particularly well with the simplicity of spirit of early Islam. The geometrical and plant forms and the Kufic or cursive script provided the basic motifs for the ornamental tiles.

In the wall of the mosque nearest to Mecca (the *qibla*) is the *mihrab,* a niche in the wall, which is of great religious significance. From the mihrab an *imam* leads the congregation in prayer, which for Moslems involves a number of ritually set physical movements of the body. Hence the carpeted floor is more appropriate than chairs or benches would be. To the right of the mihrab is the *minbar* (pulpit) from which the sermon is preached on Fridays, the holy day.

Left of the mihrab is a railed platform,

The Dome of the Rock of Jerusalem, the earliest mosque ever built (687–91), was constructed on a rock believed to be the spot where Mohammed ascended into heaven.

the *dikka,* supporting the *maksara* – traditionally the seat of honour for the caliph. The original purpose of the dikka was to separate the caliph from would-be attackers who might mingle with the congregation, because three of the first caliphs were assassinated, two actually in a mosque. Mosques were normally lit by lamps or candelabra which enhanced the beauty of the arcaded interiors but otherwise had no special religious significance.

The oldest existing mosque, the Dome of the Rock, in Jerusalem, built 687–91, resembles Byzantine buildings such as the church of San Vitale in Ravenna or St Sergius in Constantinople (now Istanbul). It was built on a rock that protrudes through the floor and is believed to be the spot from which Mohammed ascended to heaven. The richly gilded dome of this mosque rests on a drum having 16 windows. This structure is supported by 4 piers and 12 columns arranged in a circle to surround the rock. A comparatively low octagonal structure forms the external wall of the mosque, reaching to rather less than half the height of the dome. At

Samarra, in Iraq, where the Moslems founded a great city in the mid ninth century, they built the largest mosque ever constructed. This was patterned on the Dome of the Rock, but its minaret was a massive tapered spiral structure, recognizably copied from the Babylonian ziggurats.

The Great Mosque at Damascus, com-

Modelled like a Babylonian temple tower, this spiralling minaret is part of the Great Mosque of al-Mutawakkil. Founded in 836 in ancient Samarra, Iraq, it is the largest mosque ever built. Another early mosque, *right,* al-Azhar in Cairo, is a fine example of the Egyptian style of Islamic architecture.

pleted in 715, is in some respects even more Byzantine. Its interior walls are covered with beautiful mosaics in the stylized plant and geometrical patterns that became usual. Damascus, capital of the Syrian Umayyad dynasty, was soon rivalled by Cordoba, which became the capital of another branch of the Umayyads, based in Spain. In 785 the Umayyads founded a mosque at Cordoba that is to this day one of the most beautiful religious buildings in the world. The Cordoba mosque was further embellished during later centuries. Its special feature is its elaborately decorated, double-storeyed mihrab, added two centuries after the mosque was built.

A remarkable aspect of Islamic art was its tendency to flourish in one area while declining in another. While Moslem culture shone in Spain it declined in Egypt. Then, in 969, the Fatimids, an Arab dynasty, established an independent caliphate based on Cairo. Their dynasty, which lasted for two centuries, took the lead in Islamic culture west of Syria. In 970 they began to build al-Azhar. This mosque, which followed the standard Arab pat-

Islamic art and literature then entered its 'golden age' and Baghdad became the legendary city of the Thousand and One Nights. A slight decline set in from 1055, when the Seljuk Turks from Turkestan took the city, but a 'silver age' lasted for another two centuries until the Mongols captured Baghdad in 1258. During the whole of the Abbasid period the decorative arts flourished. Persia became the centre for crafts, including carpet-making, unsurpassed in their quality. Although human and animal motifs never appeared in mosque decoration, they became common elsewhere.

When the Mongols destroyed the already shrunken Abbasid caliphate it was by no means the end of the Islamic culture. Like the Turks, who had been moving into Anatolia from the eleventh century onwards, the Mongols adopted the Moslem religion with the result that Islam ex- **2**

1 Boldly designed and coloured, this sixteenth-century ceramic lamp was made for the most important mosque of Istanbul - the Sulaymaniyeh Cami. **2** Abstract design elements figure in fifteenth-century ceramic ware from Iran.

tern, was of massive stone construction as were most of the many other Fatimid buildings. Book-painting, in the style of Baghdad, seems to have flourished under the Fatimids, but the only surviving Fatimid paintings are on ceramic ware.

Even before the Umayyads had built their mosque in Cordoba, the Umayyad dynasty in Damascus had disappeared to be replaced by the Abbasid dynasty (750–1258), based on the new capital of Baghdad. East of Egypt and Arabia, Arab influence waned and Persian culture came increasingly to influence Islamic art.

Clear, jewel-like colours dazzle the eyes with their radiance in this lacquer-painted bookbinding of the sixteenth century from Tabriz, Iran. In that country, depiction of the human form, forbidden by strict Moslem code, was allowed in secular art.

panded rather than contracted. The Abbasid caliphate had hardly disappeared from Baghdad before Moslem traders took the faith eastwards to Sumatra, and during the next four centuries mosques began to appear throughout Indonesia. Within a century the Mongol rulers of Persia and Iraq had become patrons of the arts. They built stately mosques and their artists established the tradition of Persian miniature-painting, produced to illustrate the works of the poets. Tabriz, and later Shiraz and Herat (now in Afghanistan) became the chief centres of their beautiful miniatures, delightfully painted in startling colours often against a background of gold. The miniature-painters took a variety of themes, including courtly banquets and wine parties, hunting scenes, worship in the mosque, love episodes, activities of demons and Islamic legends.

The height of Islamic culture

In the second half of the fourteenth century yet another conqueror came from the east, Timur the Lame (Tamerlane), a Tartar, or Mongol Turk. His ruthless armies quickly overran India, Afghanistan, Persia and Syria. Yet even this apparent disaster proved to be a blessing for Islam, for Timur was not only a well-educated man who loved the arts, but also a devout Moslem. The Timurid period of Islamic culture that then began is symbolized by Timur's mausoleum at Samarkand. This beautiful mausoleum, called the *Gur Emir,* is reminiscent of the *ger* or portable felt tent of the Mongol nomads. It is basically a bulbous fluted dome with a ribbon tent-like decoration, supported by

Persian miniature-painters of the sixteenth century excelled in delicate depictions of themes from Persian literature. The hero Khusraw spies the princess Shirin bathing, in an illustration from the *Khamsa*, or Five Poems, of Nizami.

a tiled drum decorated in the Kufic script, resting on an octagonal surround. A marvellous age of Islamic culture reached its full flowering *c.* 1600 in Persia under the rule of Shah Abbas. His capital, Isfahan, became a city of unparalleled architectural beauty, so that travellers said 'Isfahan is half the world.' In Isfahan's Masjid-i-Shah (Shah Mosque), with its magnificent blue tile-work and faience mosaic, the art of the mosque reached near-perfection.

Baber, a later relative of Timur's, who seized India in 1526, set up the Mughal dynasty which gave its name to another great branch of art. Timurid-Persian art fused with native Indian art to produce the distinct Mughal style of painting and architecture – the supreme example being the Taj Mahal, the domed tomb built for Shah Jahan's wife. But Mughal art is more

Left, Dome and minarets of the Chaharbagh Mosque in Isfahan, Iran, gleam in the sun. Decorated in magnificent blue mosaic patterns traditional in Islamic architecture, such houses of prayer are to be seen all over the Moslem world. *Right,* in Bukhara in the USSR the courtyard of a *madrasah* (religious college) exhibits many characteristics of mosque architecture.

properly Indian than Islamic.

Although the Moslem faith continued to expand after 1600, Islam's great period in art was over. Moslem craftsmen still carry on minor arts, producing fine metalwork, carpets, textiles and other objects, but the remarkable achievements of Islamic art lie in the past.

Ancient arts of Central America

The Spanish *Conquistadores* came to plunder the ancient kingdoms of Central America. Subsequent research has built up a picture of these civilizations through the richness and variety of their art.

THE ARTS of the American Indians have a certain unity of character which is more marked than among any other large group of nations. This is probably due to the fact that the people had a common origin. It is possible to draw parallels between the design styles of the Indians of British Columbia and the pre-Inca civilizations of Peru, or between the Plains Indians of the Missouri and the Forest tribes of the Amazon jungle. All the diverse peoples of America tended to use symbolic outline drawings of people and objects to build patterns which are almost a form of writing.

From the first millennium B C to A D 1500 the Central American area, from Mexico to Panama, was the scene of many specialized developments in design, though the designs developed from the techniques of weaving and pottery influenced all aspects of art. The level of civilization in the area did not determine the quality of design. We find elaborately painted pottery from Panama, made by people living in small groups of villages of a Neolithic cultural level, which rivals the magnificent painted pottery made in the most sophisticated city-states of the Maya of southern Mexico.

However, over the whole area technical limitations conditioned the possibilities open to artists. There was no potter's wheel, so all pottery was made either by coiling rings of clay or moulding. There were only a few bronze tools made, and then only in western Mexico, so sculpture was almost entirely produced by means of stone tools. One true arch has been reported from an early Maya site, but the idea was not adopted, and for over 2,000 years, right up until the Spanish conquest in the sixteenth century, buildings were arranged with simple lintel and post construction.

Paper from fig trees

In the northern half of the area, a few centuries before Christ, paper was known and used. It was made from the inner bark of young branches of a type of fig tree. This material was dried first, then laid out in several layers one over the other, soaked and then thoroughly felted by beating with wood- and stone-faced mallets. This material, known in Mexico as *amatl,* was used for painted books, which were rather like long, narrow fire screens covered with pictures telling a

Many civilizations have risen and fallen in the area we know as Central America and their art remains to show us what they were like. The map pinpoints where the main developments took place. With the discovery and cultivation of maize, a regular food supply was ensured. Settled tribal groups were established and the opportunity was provided for elaborate civilizations to develop.

historical story or recounting a religious myth. Leather was also used for making books: long strips of softly tanned deerskin were coated, like the paper, with a lime wash, which was smoothed and then painted upon with a form of lamp black made from soot, and colours, most of which were mineral. Red from the cochineal insect was also important.

Painting was perhaps the most impor-

tant of the arts, since all sculpture was painted, almost all pottery, and although many good dyes were known, a number of painted textiles also survive. The ideas associated with colour were important to all the different tribes of the region. They were mostly based on sky-colours at different times of day: yellow for sunrise, blue and green for the south and the waters of fertility, red for the sunset, and black for the night and the north.

A very special form of painting was due to the typically American Indian desire for facial and body decoration. This varied from the simple stripes of red, white and black on some of the wilder tribes of the mountains in Panama, to the sophisticated stamped designs Aztec beauties used to decorate their yellow-powdered cheeks.

Gold working, which developed from about the first century A D, was restricted to two areas: Panama and Costa Rica in the south, and western Mexico in the north. The gold was not mined but was washed from stream beds. It was beaten into sheets and used for decoration in this form in both areas, and in Mexico it was cast in moulds to make small figurines and pendants. In the south the same process was used for casting, but the metallurgists of the small village communities developed more sophisticated methods. They used copper, and mixtures of copper and gold, for casting the basic forms of bells and plaques. These they enriched by washing out the surface copper with vegetable acids, or by plating with gold in a mercury amalgam from which the mercury was later driven off by heat. In both processes the surface was finished by burnishing with polished stone.

In the southern regions, the contradiction between high artistic achievement and low material culture had been noted by the Spanish conquerors soon after A D 1500. Archaeologists have shown that the local cultures had reached a greater height of sophistication between A D 1000 and 1200, before breaking down as the result of intertribal wars. However, we know little of the archaeological past of this region. Research further north has established dating sequences of greater interest.

Settled village life

Even in Mexico, where a few palaeo-Indian carvings have been found dating to about 12,000 years ago, the real development of settled communities with considerable artwork began only in the second millennium B C. This was a period of agricultural village life which produced great numbers of very attractive little pottery figures of fertility spirits. They are usually naked girls wearing elaborate hair styles and a little jewellery. Some represent a mother goddess with a baby in her arms; a few show young men. This development occurs a few centuries later in Mexico than the development of simple buildings and pottery in Peru 4,000 miles to the south.

In Central America the development of large villages practising maize culture and using decorated pottery became general at an early stage. Development into a high civilization with ceremonial buildings and developed sculpture first occurred in the region of the Olmecs in southern Vera Cruz, Mexico. These people flourished between 900 and 400 B C. Their art shows some design elements which may have derived from the Mexican plateau in earlier times. In later times, after Olmec art had left Mexico, there are similar designs on pottery of the early centuries A D from the Mississippi valley.

An Olmex clay head from Mexico.

The Olmec use of relief carving set in a decorative pattern of lines is apparently unique in Mexico, though in the overall field of American Indian art it is apparent from Peru to Alaska, and rather specially in the quite recent art of the carvers of totem poles in British Columbia. The Olmecs showed great skill in carving hard stones such as basalt and jade. Some of the themes of their sculpture – the jaguar-man, the Earth-dragon – recur throughout later

The Zapotecs of central Mexico made pottery figures of deities to stand at the entrance of tombs as guardian spirits. These were often in the shape of urns bearing offerings to the god.

Central American art. They express a typical group of religious ideas for the area. Another great step forward by the Olmec artists around 900 B C was the development of symbolic glyphs to form a kind of syllabic writing. The system developed in a simple form among the Zapotecs of Oaxaca in Mexico from 200 B C onwards, and they continued to decorate their famous pottery urns with symbols which were the names of their gods.

Zapotec arts are characterized by their use of applied decoration on pottery, the simple strong construction of their jade ornaments, and the powerful simplicity of their architecture at such sites as Monte Alban and Mitla. Their painting was, as far as we knew it, large in scale and uncomplicated when compared with the pictorial styles of surrounding peoples. They remained independent from the first few centuries B C to about A D 1480. The style of their art suffered no basic changes, though fashion was affected from time to time by the art of which ever people were dominant upon the neighbouring Mexican plateau.

South of Mexico and throughout San Salvador, Guatemala and parts of Nicaragua lived the Maya people. From the village communities of the second century B C developed a series of powerful and highly civilized city-states which began to erect great buildings and monumental stelae (stone pillars often used as grave stones) in the second century A D. These talented people reached their artistic zenith in the seventh and eighth centuries when their art was showing all the characteristics of the Baroque style of the seventeenth century in Europe in its love

A detail from the *Borbonicus codex*, depicting part of the Maya calendar. Each day is guarded by gods: here Tezcatlitoca, god of all things of this world, wears the human skin of a sacrificial victim as the plumed serpent, also the green Earth, receives the body.

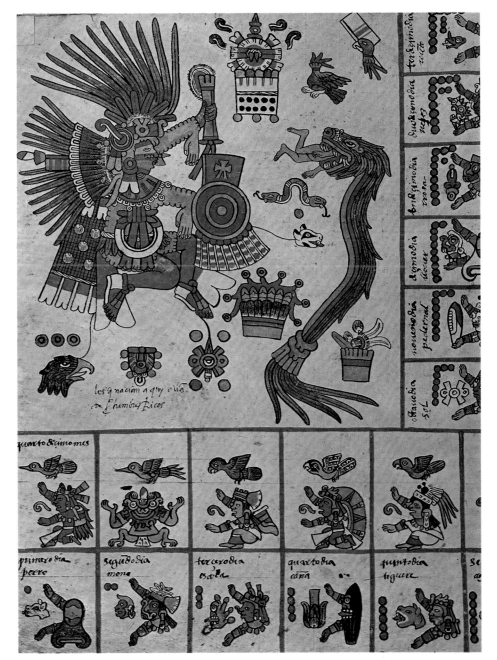

los q̃ nacian a q̃ny eñã
en ʒhombuʒ bicoʒ

only three late examples survive. Their buildings were of lintel and post construction, and the temples were erected at the tops of huge pyramidal mounds which were also decorated with paintings. Temple buildings were heavily sculpted and, like all Maya constructions, they were elaborately painted in fresco.

In the early tenth century the Maya culture collapsed, and a rather more simple form of life and art developed in a revived Maya culture in the Yucatan Peninsula. Here it was greatly influenced by an invasion of Mexican Toltec clans who built a Mexican-style city at Chichen Itza soon

1 Maya maize god from Copan, Honduras. The Maya, worked largely in stone. **2** Innumerable *stelae,* or pillars, were erected to mark steps in the complicated Maya calendar.

of decoration and flowing forms.

They achieved what appears to be true portraiture both in modelled stucco and in small clay figurines. Their painting rapidly developed from the formalism of pottery design to fresco, in which large groups of people could be shown in true spatial relationships and figures could be foreshortened. The frescoes at Bonampak are the most important witness to this unique achievement of American Indian painting.

Pyramid temples

The Maya developed a syllabic form of writing with about 700 glyphs, which appear in sculpture, pottery, wall painting and on the books of prophecy of which

Quetzalcoatl is the plumed serpent, fierce-looking yet gentle god of Central American civilizations. Here serpent-pillars rear up at the approach to the Temple of the Warriors at Chichen Itza.

after AD 1000. The Maya achieved complete independence by AD 1350, but continuous dynastic wars prevented them from achieving the high cultural levels of their ancestors. However the late Maya produced the books of Maya religion which have survived until the present day.

To the west of the Maya were the Pipiles, who appear to have been moving northwards along the Pacific coast in the early centuries AD, bringing a new art style and a system of written dates, first to the coasts of San Salvador and then to Guatemala. At Sta Lucia Cotzumahualpa their artists carved large reliefs depicting astronomical events. The stelae on which these lively works were carved have yielded dates as early as the fifth century AD. When this new art style reached southern Mexico in the seventh century AD, it began to replace the arts of the great city of Teotihuacan on the Mexican plateau.

Teotihuacan was a metropolis which had influenced art styles throughout Mexico from the second century BC until the fifth century AD. Its characteristic pottery figurines were well modelled, though formal in pattern. Painting was highly symbolic, and is confined to flat wash drawing within black formal outlines. Pottery was incised with symbols, and sometimes even frescoed with colours painted over a coating of lime. Teotihuacano art spread to northern and eastern Mexico, and in Guatemala it reached along the Pacific coast to the mountains on the edge of the Maya country. The great city of nearly a million inhabitants fell, as it rose, for unknown reasons about AD 600. Its art disappeared, though many of the symbols can be seen in new adaptations in later art.

A period of disorganization followed the fall of Teotihuacan, but many art styles, mostly of formal design and elaborate symbolism, flourished. Notable among them were those associated with the sites of Xochicalco and Tajin. However after a

A funerary mask decorated largely in soft jade mosaic from the mysterious city of Teotihuacan on the Mexican plateau.

time the Toltecs gained ascendancy and established a kind of leadership of the country from their city at Tula. They used the calendar of the Pipiles, and their art styles show many characteristics of that people. The Toltecs were remarkable for the development of palace building around courtyards, and for the concept of the temple as only part of the building complex. Their art is strictly formal, and in many ways glorifies the military deities. Their traders penetrated far and brought turquoise from New Mexico, and imported golden ornaments from Panama. They were the first people to use metal tools in Mexico.

The Toltec ascendancy lasted from about A D 750 until late in the ninth century. After their capital was destroyed in a civil war, some of their leaders migrated to Chichen Itza in Yucatan and built there a Toltec city which decisively influenced Maya art.

After the fall of Tula, many Toltec traditions were continued by the Mixtec, a people of the mountains of Oaxaca. To the Mixtecs we are indebted for most of the surviving painted books of Mexican tradition. These are painted in black outline with many-coloured filling-in on lime-washed strips of tanned skin. They can now be read, and many of the historical records take us back well into Toltec times.

Some religious books in this artistic tradition derived from the Toltecs seem

A common motif in Mexican art is the serpent, which symbolized strength, wisdom, the Earth, fire. A turquoise ornament, probably Mixtec.

to have originated from other tribes in central and southern Mexico, but the tradition is so strong that it may well be that Mixtec artists were employed either as painters or teachers. The later Aztecs admitted their cultural debts to the Mixtecs in all fields of art.

War and sacrifice

The Aztecs rose to power only in the thirteenth century. They were contemporaries of the great Inca kingdom in Peru, but in all probability neither civilization had heard of the other.

Little of their textile art has survived, but painted books give clues to the brilliance and beauty of their woven cloth. They also made most elaborate garments and headdresses from the coloured feathers of tropical birds. Of these, half a dozen examples remain in European museums to testify to the wonders of this art. Their craftsmen under Mixtec instruction produced objects covered with micro-mosaics of turquoise and other semi-precious stones. Wood carving reached a high standard and was often partially gilded. Pottery also became more and more re-

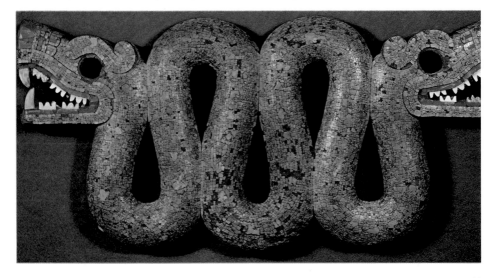

The Aztecs were the last civilization to rise to power in Mexico before the Spanish Conquest. In architecture they based their style on half-forgotten Tolmec traditions, but in sculpture they made notable advances. *Left*, a stone statue of Xiuhtecuhtli, god of fire.

fined in the hands of the craftsmen and women of Mexico City, which was built on the site of the Aztec city of Tenochtitlán.

The brilliant achievements of the Aztecs were eclipsed by the Spanish invasion of 1518–21. Afterwards, terrible epidemics of smallpox reduced the population to a fifth of the former number. In the Spanish Colonial period, however, Aztec artists still worked on church sculpture and carving, giving a special flavour to the Mexican versions of Spanish Baroque and Churrigueresque art which had taken over the whole of Central American culture. It was only after the revolution of 1911 in Mexico that the real understanding of ancient arts could be achieved. The artists of modern Mexico acknowledge a great debt to the American Indian ancestors of their people, and have produced fine modern work which is the more vigorous because it derives both from Indian and European traditions.

Index

'p' after a page number means there is a relevant illustration on that page
'c' after a page number means there is relevant material in a caption on that page

63